丝绸的故事

Customs, Traditions and Landmarks |
Non-Fiction Series

Copyright © 2022 by Level Learning, INC. and Washington Yu Ying PCS™
Original and Edited Text Copyright © 2022 by Washington Yu Ying PCS™

All rights reserved. No part of this book in whole or part may be reproduced without written permission from the publisher.

Published by Level Learning, INC.

Content Contributors:
Washington Yu Ying PCS™
Level Learning - Ya-Ching Chang

Illustrations by: Josh Taira

Leveling classification based on Level Learning standard.
For full description, visit www.levellearning.com

ISBN 978-1-64040-024-5
Simplified Chinese Edition

About Level Learning:
Level Learning provides a literacy focused curriculum specifically designed for K-12 Chinese as a Second Language classrooms. Our program offers 20 levels of specific and detailed objectives, leveled texts and passages, mastery-based online assessment, and analytics to enable data-driven instruction. Level Learning reading curriculum for both literature and informational text emphasize grammar and comprehension skills to help teachers develop confident and independent Chinese language readers. The non-fiction series of books are specifically designed to support our informational text course based on multiple national standards. To learn more about our entire offering, visit www.levellearning.com.

About Washington Yu Ying PCS™:
Washington Yu Ying PCS is a Mandarin English dual language immersion International Baccalaureate (IB) World school. Yu Ying's mission is to inspire and prepare young people to create a better world by challenging them to reach their full potential in a nurturing Chinese/English educational environment. Yu Ying's comprehensive IB, dual immersion curriculum equips students with global competencies for success in the real world. As a leader in immersion education, Yu Ying is determined to advance Chinese language programs and global citizenry education by helping other schools create and strengthen their Chinese programs. For more information, email: products@washingtonyuying.org

很多人到中国玩，都会买丝绸作为纪念品。用蚕丝做的丝绸，摸起来又柔软又舒服。

用蚕丝做成的丝绸，可以用来做衣服、丝巾、被子等。早在五千年前，中国人就会用蚕丝做衣服了。

传说嫘祖是最早用蚕丝做衣服的人。

有一天，嫘祖在桑树下喝茶。突然，有个东西掉进她的杯子里。

嫘祖拿起这个东西，拉出了一条蚕丝。她发现这条蚕丝可以拉得很长，而且不容易断。于是，嫘祖就想到了用蚕丝做衣服。

后来，嫘祖教人们种桑树和养蚕。她也教人们用蚕丝做衣服。

蚕丝做的衣服穿起来又柔软又舒服。而且蚕丝染上不同的颜色以后,看起来非常漂亮。

渐渐地，蚕丝做的丝绸变得非常有名。那时候，只有中国才有丝绸。汉朝的时候，中国的丝绸开始卖到世界其他国家。

丝绸之路

后来,人们把运送丝绸的路称为"丝绸之路"。

直到现在,中国的丝绸还是非常有名。很多人到中国玩,都会买丝绸作为纪念。

Glossary

	Pinyin	English Definition
买	mǎi	to buy
丝绸	sī chóu	silk
纪念品	jì niàn pǐn	souvenir
蚕丝	cán sī	silk from silkworm
摸	mō	to touch
柔软	róu ruǎn	soft
舒服	shū fu	comfortable
丝巾	sī jīn	scarf
被子	bèi zi	quilt
传说	chuán shuō	legend
嫘祖	léi zǔ	a Chinese empress, wife of the Yellow Emperor
桑树	sāng shù	mulberry tree
喝茶	hē chá	to drink tea
掉进	diào jìn	to fall into
断	duàn	broken

	Pinyin	English Definition
种	zhòng	to grow
养蚕	yǎng cán	to raise silkworms
渐渐地	jiàn jiàn de	slowly, gradually
有名	yǒu míng	famous
汉朝	hàn cháo	Han Dynasty
丝绸之路	sī chóu zhī lù	The Silk Road

www.ingramcontent.com/pod-product-compliance
Lightning Source LLC
Chambersburg PA
CBHW041221070526
44584CB00001B/48